A

OF
DEPRESSION

Gary H. Lovejoy, PhD

wphonline.com

Copyright © 2014 by Gary H. Lovejoy and Gregory M. Knopf
Published by Wesleyan Publishing House
Indianapolis, Indiana 46250
Printed in the United States of America
ISBN: 978-0-89827-830-9
ISBN (e-book): 978-0-89827-831-6

This book contains advice and information relating to physical and
mental health and medicine. It is not intended to replace professional
advice and should be used to supplement rather than replace regular
care by your physician or other professional care provider. Readers
are encouraged to consult their physicians with specific questions
and concerns.

CONTENTS

FOREWORD

If you want advice about fixing your car, you seek an experienced mechanic; if you want advice about selling your home, you seek a successful real estate agent; and if you want to know more about the weather, you seek the reports of a trained meteorologist. But if you want to understand something as deeply personal as your experience with depression, you would seek not merely a competent therapist, but one whose mature Christian faith is evident and whose values are similar to your own. In all the years I have known him (and that goes back to our college days together), Dr. Gary Lovejoy is just such a person. His unwavering belief in God's healing power, deep love for people, intellectual curiosity, and understanding of the paradoxical traps others find themselves in makes him uniquely compassionate about the Christian's struggle with depression.

Always a man to thoroughly prepare himself for something, Gary is well-educated and trained as a therapist who systematically explores every dimension of a problem. After many years of private practice, in which he has counseled several thousand depressed people, many of them believers, Gary has come to some important conclusions about integrating spiritual and emotional insights that reframe the issues clients most often struggle with. In *Light in the Darkness: Finding Hope in the Shadow of Depression*, Gary answers the question that is so commonly found on the lips of troubled Christians about how to relate their depressive experience to their faith. By identifying how depression, like anger and fear, is a key emotional alarm system, signaling that something in life needs our attention, he has removed the stigma so many people have placed on emotional struggles.

Now, in *A Pastor's Guide for the Shadow of Depression*, Gary addresses the topic of depression in the unique circumstances and often unrealistic expectations of pastoral ministry. Not only does he help pastors recognize when they may be depressed, he also gives practical guidance on how pastors can address issues proactively to minimize the risk of depression.

All in all, this short book should be available for reference in every pastor's study. Besides being a great read, it is an invaluable aid in keeping our heads straight about God's view of our struggles. I could not recommend it more highly.

Dr. Gary Smalley
author and speaker on family relationships

1

UNDERSTANDING PASTORS AND DEPRESSION

Have you ever asked yourself, "Why am I beating my head against the wall—what does God want from me anyway?" Have you thought to yourself, "I'm so tired of this; all I wanted to do was to serve God and teach his Word"?

If, as a church pastor, you've ever had these or similar thoughts, you're definitely not alone.

When you are called to the pastorate, you enter an especially demanding and emotionally challenging ministry. It's demanding because pastors are too often expected to be all things to all people. They are expected to be inspiring preachers, guiding shepherds, savvy administrators, wise counselors who are always available, and more generally, paragons of Solomonic wisdom. They are expected to be gifted theologians, crisis management experts, models of emotional stability and spiritual health, and problem-solving savants in the church community. What's more, they are charged with presiding over a wide range of imperfect (and sometimes contentious) people, some of whom represent vexing problems to the pastor.

Yet pastors are themselves flawed and limited human beings who cannot reasonably be expected to perfectly fulfill every role the congregation implicitly demands. Since most pastors are not equally gifted to excel in all things, some tasks will be more daunting than others. For instance, not all pastors are especially gifted in counseling, but they are nonetheless often required to spend a lot of their time doing it. That's because many people seek out their pastors first when they are encountering personal crises they cannot resolve on their own.

As a pastor, you usually don't have the luxury of picking and choosing the roles you wish to take. Try it and you'll likely encounter pushback from the board and grumbling from the congregation. Generally speaking, pastors walk a fine line between fulfilling well-established expectations and introducing new ideas of ministry. One serious misstep and you may very well find yourself in that dreaded zone of adversarial conflict— the kind that reminds you just how easy it is to become the center of a storm.

Leading a church is never the simple, unified task some think it to be. It sometimes calls for a level of emotional strength exceeding that which the pastor can provide. Studies show that a great majority of pastors consider resigning from the ministry at some point or another during their careers. Indeed, over 50 percent of them do. Studies also show that roughly seven out of ten pastors suffer from depression, sometimes profound depression.[1] Yet most of them suffer in agonizing silence, fearful that their despair is a sure sign that they have somehow failed to be the stalwart fortress of strength they were called to be. What's more, in their minds, they have failed to set the example of peace expected from one presumed to be living the abundant life in Christ. It is little wonder that they are often ashamed they are depressed.

So they routinely disguise it, privately pleading with God to help them control their terrifying implosion, to heal them from the fatal flaw of despair that threatens their ministry. They fear being unmasked as a spiritual fraud, a failure to God . . . and to themselves. They instruct their assistants to shield them from the flow of those needing something from them by redirecting church members to others deemed more capable of handling the load. They talk about physically not feeling very well and that they just need more rest. Usually, the congregation is in the dark as to the real reason why the pastor is missing from the pulpit. Rather, they are told that the pastor is sick or exhausted and to pray for healing.

Anytime I speak to a congregation, when I look across the sea of faces, I know that a high percentage of them are probably going through difficult times and may be struggling with some level of depression. And that may be true even when they reply "Fine" to the ritual inquiry about how things are going. People in general and Christians in particular are often experts at pretense. They don't want others to know what's going on . . . unless they can really trust the person they're talking to, and even then they're often reluctant to disclose their despair.

The statistics consistently tell us that the majority of hurting congregation members have not sought help for their struggle. So there they sit in the pew, in their private world of pain, looking at the pastor but with their minds fixed on an internal warfare far from the topic at hand. The pastor's familiar challenge is to say something that will bridge to that world of pain, bring their attention back to God's desire to heal their wounds, and let them know they aren't alone in the battle.

But I'm also aware of something equally important. There are pastors who faithfully lead these congregations of hurting people. Yet how many think about the burden pastors must bear? Who addresses how they are doing? Are there confidants to share their burdens? Are there "Tituses" to bring encouragement and provide needed perspective? The pastor is expected to minister to others, but who is there to minister to the pastor?

This guide is intended to be a step in that direction.

CONFRONTING THE PREJUDICE AGAINST DEPRESSION

Many pastors (and their congregations) believe that it's possible they can fall victim to almost any affliction, except depression. Among Christians, there appears to be a genuine prejudice with regard to fellow believers who are depressed. As one psychologist put it, it's the only affliction with physical and emotional characteristics that has spiritual implications as well. It's an unwritten rule that people don't want their pastors spiritually victimized or weakened. If they view depression as a failure to live victoriously in the faith, then it's not hard to see why depression is the last thing they expect in their spiritual leader.

Unfortunately, most pastors buy into this point of view. When they become depressed, they are not merely in emotional pain; they're also in denial. Clearly, they find their struggle fundamentally unacceptable. To them, it's not only incomprehensible that they're depressed, it's horrifying and humiliating, especially if they have always believed that it's a sign of spiritual weakness. Yet even though they remain in searing pain, spiraling ever downward, they still have an "image" to keep up. They also have church responsibilities that continue to stare them in the face.

What usually follows is an elaborate cover-up that only further isolates the pastor and confuses the congregation.

Under these conditions, the depression grows even darker, perhaps to a level that is intolerable to keep functioning as a shepherd to a spiritually needy flock. Pastors who get to this point usually feel completely defeated. It rarely occurs to them that God could use them even more powerfully for the kingdom precisely because they know what it's like to grapple with depression. Instead, some—especially those who believe they have somehow failed God—leave the ministry altogether, never to return. Some are even bitter, thinking God abandoned them in their hour of greatest need.

It doesn't have to be this way. Indeed, judging from his response to his servants in the Bible, God wants something entirely different for his beloved. He wants his servants to fully experience his mercy and compassion, to grow through their pain so as to serve him more knowledgably. He already knows that those who follow him will, at times, become emotionally overwhelmed by what life throws at them. To God, that's not a sign of failure; it's a sign of humanity living in a broken world.

King David cried out many times in utter despair. But it was in his despair that he really learned the meaning of God's grace, which enabled him to do great things for the kingdom. After all, he was called a man after God's own heart—not because he was a king who conquered his enemies, but because he allowed himself to be shaped by God through his despair over adversity. Taken together, David's psalms are an exquisite example of this honing process.

THE CHALLENGE OF SELF-DISCLOSURE

When pastors feel defeated, it is usually because they have long held the pain in because of misguided notions about their positions as church leaders. But on the rare occasions when pastors do open up to their congregations about struggles with depression, they are often surprised to discover just how many of the flock are going through a similar battle. They are also introduced to the reality that they likewise have been driven into silence and pretense by feelings of guilt and shame. When they share their stories, not only does it create an instant connection with these wounded souls, but it also forges a bond of relief from the self-loathing that comes with being depressed in the first place.

Some time ago, a local pastor in my city revealed to his congregation that he had been, for a considerable period of time, fighting severe depression. He was shocked by how many came to him after that church service to offer their support and to share their own stories of pain. Many had kept these stories secret for years out of fear of appearing spiritually inferior. This moment of pastoral candor began a remarkable revival of transparency in the church that lifted them to a new level of fellowship. They subsequently became a powerful draw to the rest of the community, growing at a rate they had not witnessed in a very long time.

One of the reasons depression has become the "hidden disorder" among Christians is because it's rarely a sermon topic in the church. Many pastors simply seem reticent to preach on it. In contacting churches to introduce them to our (Gregory Knopf, MD, and myself) seminar on depression (called "Breakthrough: Journey out of Depression"), we were surprised to find a large number who were cool to our invitation. Unfortunately, silence on the subject implicitly conveys the message that depression is not common enough in the Christian community, nor a topic that is frequent enough in the Bible, to merit much attention. This message, which can sometimes be a product of the pastor's own fears, only deepens the depressed believer's sense of isolation.

Those who enter God's house burdened with despair are often convinced that they must be out of touch with the spiritual mainstream of the church. This naturally leads them to believe that their mood disorder must be evidence of sin or at least insufficient faith. Unfortunately, those who contend that spiritually mature Christians never have a reason to be depressed reinforce this view. But their arguments ignore the many cases of depression found among God's servants in the Bible. They also ignore the record of God's redemptive responses to these emotional downturns.

By dismissing—either directly or indirectly—the importance of discussing depression among believers, we inadvertently convey either a profound fear of emotional disorders or a naïve view of the Christian life as one without struggle. Ironically, such views are a common *source* of depression, because they lead to a persistent sense of hopelessness about ever pleasing God. This is all the more the case when adversity strikes, as it sooner or later will.

When pastors embrace a rationale that prohibits admitting depression or seeking counsel for it, they find that they have nowhere else to go to find relief. Take this pastor's story:

Trying to handle depression alone is its own type of insanity. One of the things I eventually learned is that recovering from depression requires lots of help from other people. In fact, my martyr-like approach to the problem, had I stayed with it, could have been disastrous. . . . But I didn't realize that at the time. Besides, I was afraid that people would see me as weak if they discovered that I struggled with it—that the stresses of planting a church and functioning as a pastor were too much for me. . . .

Letting others help was pivotal in my healing. To my surprise, most people actually felt closer to me, even energized by the opportunity to help their pastor. . . . Some pastors struggle with the appropriateness of receiving help that isn't exclusively theological or specifically scriptural in approach. Others are so used to being the ones giving help that they find it difficult to receive any. And of course, some question the ministry of Christian therapy altogether. I was a member of the second and third groups—especially the third. "The Scriptures are my therapist," I would say, "and they don't charge me $100 per hour for the service."

Certainly, the Bible contributed much to my recovery. . . . But being forced by my circumstances to ask for help from an able counselor changed my entire outlook. Without that wonderful man's prayer, honest questioning, and practical help, I don't know how long it would have taken me to heal, or if ever I *would* have. I continue to find strength and guidance from the Word of God. But in it I read about the importance of Christian community in discerning the deep things of the Spirit. . . .

While I'm certainly not claiming amazing humility, I can sure say that I'm a softer, more broken person than I used to be. That was God's gift to me and our church—one that resulted from being temporarily defeated by depression."[2]

This pastor went on to describe more specifically how this God-given gift had changed him and consequently lifted his church. One church member even said to him, "I've noticed that something has changed in you. You're not nearly so threatening as you used to be. I think I'm ready to get more involved in the church now."[3]

A REASON FOR HOPE

The reason we more accurately describe depression as an emotional alarm system signaling the need for change of some sort is because it helps us to understand its design in prompting an intervention that will prove to be healing to our hearts and minds. Rather than fearing or rejecting emotional turmoil, we are invited to use it to discover something important about ourselves or our circumstances. In the process, we are given the opportunity to learn more about God's abiding love for us. Contrary to rejecting depression as a sign of spiritual failure, we are challenged to address problems that may well have gone underground and been long hidden from our awareness. It can be our chance to grow in unanticipated ways. It can also force us, as it did the pastor above, to recognize that healing often comes only *after* we reach out to others for help.

How are the seeds of future depression sown? Well, we don't help matters by failing to heed the importance of building a defense against emotional collapse. Pastors, no less than their congregations, can ill afford to ignore the principles of cultivating sound mental health. Yet the demands of the church can so easily drown out the voice of reason.

It is to these factors that we now turn.

NOTES

1. Richard J. Krejcir, "Statistics on Pastors: What Is Going on with the Pastors in America?" Francis A. Schaeffer Institute of Church Leadership Development, 2007, accessed April 8, 2014, http://www.intothy word.org/apps/articles/ ?articleid=36562.

2. Art Greco, "The Monster in My Closet: A Story of Depression," *The Covenant Companion*, September 2004, 8–9, 21.

3. Ibid., 21.

THE IMPORTANCE
OF KNOWING YOURSELF

"Know thyself" is the axiom defining one of the necessary conditions for a coherent life. It's fundamental to a spiritually prosperous ministry. In one sense, it's a reflection of how you've been shaped by the hope that is within you. In another sense, it means having a clear identity—knowing who you are as a child of God—which includes your strengths as well as your weaknesses, values and convictions, and roles as pastor, spouse, parent, and friend. This presumes that you acknowledge the importance of the emotional boundaries separating these roles.

It's important to point out, for example, that you can be successful in your leadership role as a pastor (as measured by, say, growth of the church) but deficient in your role as a spouse or parent. Likewise, you can be a respected biblical scholar and teacher while at the same time languishing in your spiritual and emotional life. It is remarkably easy to descend into this kind of double life—a public one and a private one—especially when others have high expectations of you.

I have counseled numerous adult children of pastors and seminary professors over the years who disliked what they had seen as the "deceptive" spirituality of their parents. They often failed to see the deeper internal threats and conflicts of purpose which their parents were facing at the time. Instead, they privately saw unrestrained anger, marriage conflicts, and obsessions about control and image-making that ran contrary to everything they heard from their parent in the pulpit. They were repulsed by the idea that you must live a duplicitous life in which you present a false image publically in order to be a successful pastor. As a result, they were determined to have greater honesty in their own lives, even if they didn't really know what that looked like beyond simple rebellion.

KNOWING YOUR CONCEPT OF SELF

Really knowing and respecting yourself—what psychologists refer to as "self-esteem"—means, in part, that there is no need for the double life because you feel the freedom to live authentically before others. This comes from examining yourself and truly accepting the person you see because ultimately you know that you are the unique handiwork of God. Such acceptance is neither narcissism nor human pride, but rather the humble acknowledgement of God's goodness poured out in your person. It points to God's authorship, not to something of your own creation. When you understand this reality, you are ready to acknowledge your shortcomings and the full implications of your sin without rejecting yourself in the process. Self-acceptance, then, is the precondition for realizing your full potential as God's spiritual child.

Central to this perspective is the distinction between person and behavior. You can fully accept who you are without always accepting how you behave. In fact, self-respect is what most prompts your desire to change any behavior that might be damaging to a spiritually healthy way of living. It certainly doesn't mean resigning yourself to normalizing sin in your life. This is in perfect alignment with the full meaning of God's unconditional love: Because he loves you, he not only calls you to repent, but also immediately forgives you when you do. That's because he wants you to be free to live openly. He knows that a secret life of self-doubt and self-hatred will merely compromise your every attempt to live courageously. Such compromise inevitably ends in a full-scale retreat from a principled witness to God's goodness.

The apostle Paul intrinsically understood this principle when he lamented his persistent sin (the "war within his members") despite his fervent desire to live righteously (see

Rom. 7). But rather than concluding his words of frustration with a proclamation of worthlessness regarding his person, he broke out in a doxology to God's marvelous grace in Christ. He knew that divine love conquered all, even the spiritual failures of his own human nature. This is the essence of redemption itself. Life in Christ is meant to evoke a hymn of celebration not a requiem for self-victimization. Your sin, therefore, can never be the justification for self-hatred.

If you truly want to see yourself through God's eyes, to have an accurate concept of who you are, then you must see your infinite value to him. You may have heard this many times in seminary or church, but intellectual knowledge is no substitute for the experiential reality of actually beholding yourself with the same loving eyes as your Savior. Only then is the question of your worth a settled issue. It's never been about your performance. Instead, it's about unselfcon-sciously serving others. As author Kenneth Blanchard put it in an interview, your life is "not about thinking less of your-self, but about thinking of yourself less"[1] . . . and (I would add) is what frees you to think of others more. That's why the Bible defines humility as an attitude of service to others based on a sense of personal worth affirmed by Christ's sac-rifice and a sense of initiative empowered by the Holy Spirit. This is the other-centered nature of agape love in action, a love which turns us outward toward others, not inward toward the self.

You have been taught, and no doubt have preached, that what matters to God should matter to us. We are told in the opening chapter of Genesis that God values his creation of humans more highly than any other aspect of the created order. Indeed, it was only after he created humanity that he evaluated all he had made as *very* good. Each one of us, by virtue of being "made in God's likeness" (James 3:9), is not to be cursed, but treated with respect and dignity. So shouldn't we do the same and value who we are in him?

KNOWING YOUR VULNERABILITY TO MORAL TRAPS

Like many congregation members, one of the reasons pastors sometimes lose their way is that they are already lost due to a painful past. There are times when family history has wrapped its poisonous fingers around their hearts, twisting their logic into the warped reasoning of the damaged child inside. As a result, success becomes to them merely the temporary prelude to failure, setbacks become the confirmation of their incompetence, and invitations to closer relationships become threats to their vulnerability.

Performance becomes the all-absorbing focus. They long to be loved for who they are. But frankly, they don't expect it. Instead, they pin their hopes on being loved for what they do. If that doesn't work out, there's little left but despondency, usually with a residue of bitterness as well. Sadly, the failure to emancipate from a dysfunctional home has derailed many dedicated pastors with chronic depression and relational upheaval.

This includes marriages that cannot withstand the stresses of ministry and therefore begin to come apart at the seams. Crumbling marriages become the context for further anger and guilt, yet another source of despair. It's during these times that a pastor can become more vulnerable to the self-medicating attractions of someone else, often an admirer in the church. It's one of the reasons pastors are cautioned not to counsel or work alone with someone of the opposite sex. It's also true that high profile people are often targets for the affections of others who, for various reasons, feel insignificant in their own marriages and who therefore project their feelings onto idealized images of leaders. Especially when pastors are in emotionally dangerous places, this can spiral downward into very dark places, all while the public face of piety defies the sin and misery within. You have heard the stories of such tragedies, each one telling us of the heartbreak of splintered lives.

Much the same can be said of the problem of pornography among Christian leaders. It may seem scandalous to the congregation that anyone on the pastoral staff might be struggling with pornography. Yet, over the years, I have counseled not only pastors and elders but many other Christians grappling with this issue. Several years ago, a hotel chain reported that, during an annual conference for church leaders held at one of their locations, they recorded a spike in X-rated movies viewed privately in the attendees' rooms.

Unfortunately, the shame and secrecy of such a struggle only compounds the addictive nature of this behavior. There seems to be a critical period for developing this addiction spanning roughly the ages of six or seven to around fifteen. If they are exposed to pornographic materials during this period of childhood, when neural tracts for sexual development are being laid down in the brain, they will likely become trapped in this addiction indefinitely. That is, of course, unless they seek professional help for it. God does not condemn them. Instead, he desires their liberation—or, as Jesus said to the adulteress, that they "go and sin no more" (John 8:11 TLB).

Pastors must deal with seductive enticements in their own lives before they can effectively tackle those in the church. It's no accident that even Jesus had to conquer personal temptation before he took on the challenge of confronting the sin of all humanity. Without examining the quality of your own inner life, you cannot have the moral authority to encourage right living in others. This may mean revisiting experiences that you had little or no understanding of as a child, but which you can process differently now. The alternative is being stuck in cycles of secret addiction and persistent depression.

When the edifice of self-acceptance has been obliterated as a result of a person's painful history, it becomes especially difficult to embrace a loving, grace-giving God beyond the cognitive belief in the concept. It's easier to privately believe that you've been redeemed more out of divine pity (which is often how grace is mistakenly defined) than because of how much you mean to him. It's no surprise that if your thinking is dominated by lies about yourself, it's probably susceptible to lies about God as well.

While pastors have acquired great knowledge concerning the nature of God, they can nonetheless underestimate just how much their own histories have impacted their ability to internalize it. That's why knowing a lot about God does not necessarily translate into change about how they think about themselves. This can be seen, for instance, in their defensiveness or controlling tactics when others happen to disagree with them. It's one of the ways they unwittingly reveal their insecurity, rooted in their underlying struggle to accept their own legitimacy.

Unattended wounds festering deep under the surface inevitably wear down the brave façade of peace and reassurance believed necessary for a minister who wishes to portray the mind of God. Pastors so bedeviled by internal contradictions soon find their emotional resources exhausted. Though it may be euphemistically called "burnout," they're often troubled by feelings of hypocrisy.

It's only when the truth of God's Word is internalized by the optimism of redemption that pastors are in a position to see the progress they're making in their daily walk with Christ.

KNOWING YOUR PURPOSE

In addition to identity issues and self attitudes, knowing yourself also means having a distinct understanding of your goals in life (your sense of mission), your experience of God's will, and what you see as God's desire for the church. Without clear convictions in these matters, you will become adrift in a sea of ambiguity and aimlessness. As a consequence, your life and ministry will cease to make much sense, much less have any identifiable purpose. Your congregation may feel that something is out of sync, even if they may assume you have an objective to what you're doing. The danger of this disconnect is that, without concrete goals, the emotional energy of the congregation is likely to turn in a negative direction—in damaging conflicts with one another and with you as their pastor.

Goals often arise from the nature of a believer's call to the pastorate. Some pastors enter the ministry because others who took interest in the sincerity of their faith suggested it. It could have been their youth pastor or some other leader influential in their lives. Others enter the ministry because of the excitement of their newfound faith. Still others begin their seminary education uncertain of their direction, but later choose the pastorate because it seems like the best option. While the motivating conditions vary considerably, usually the commitment is made quite earnestly. That doesn't mean, however, all are best suited for the pastorate.

The seminary has, I believe, a moral obligation to discern the most capable pastoral candidates early in their education and training. Students need to be counseled regarding their aptitude and temperament for pastoral responsibilities. Too many are passed through their seminary education without much guidance only to discover later that their work in the church seems overwhelming to them. They may become disillusioned because the stresses of church administration and the disturbing malaise of a shrinking, halfhearted congregation have taken their toll. They often become first puzzled and then depressed about the apparent ineffectiveness of their ministries. Some even resign in defeat, wondering bitterly where God was in all of it.

Does this mean that their call to ministry was a false one or at least a misunderstood one?

In a few cases, it may be true that they mistook zeal for an explicit call from God. But many others, including those whose ministries have floundered, may have been unable to discern more precisely what God's call meant. At the time, there may not have been anyone to give them direction.

I remember a young man a number of years ago who was convinced he was called to go to the mission field. He had a close friend who was particularly gifted in linguistic ability and who could already speak several languages. This friend had gone into missions and served with Wycliffe Bible Translators, working among the Indian tribes in the remote and mountainous regions of Mexico. After providing these people for the first time with a written language of their own, whole tribes converted to Christianity in a powerful display of the gospel. The young man learned about these exciting results from his friend and was even more enthused about heading to the mission field. He continued to pray and seek every opportunity to apply to various mission boards for acceptance.

After being turned down by numerous boards, he became increasingly frustrated and depressed that his aspirations were being blocked and wondered why God was not opening the doors of opportunity. He remained agitated over this for many months until one day he had a conversation with his pastor which led to an entirely new insight. This young man had an uncanny ability to make money . . . lots of it. He was often described by others as having "the Midas touch." But he didn't care about wealth; all he wanted to do was go to the mission field.

However, his pastor had asked him whether he had considered the possibility that, perhaps, the call he felt was not to go to the mission field himself, but instead to financially support others to go. That was his "Aha!" moment. He concluded that God had indeed gifted him with the ability to generate great wealth and was asking him now to use it to spread the gospel through missions. At last he had peace. Over time, he came to fully financially support over a dozen missionaries, while he himself continued to live quite modestly, not wanting to waste a single penny that otherwise could go to furthering the gospel.

To this story, I could add my own experience. As a graduate student, I felt God wanted me to attend seminary. I was not sure why, though I had a strong faith and wanted to serve God. Many thought I was preparing for the pastorate. When I graduated from seminary, I still didn't know why God wanted me there, except that somehow he would use that training. In any case, I planned to go on to get my doctorate in psychology, which is what I subsequently did.

After completing my education, I taught psychology at the college level for many years as well as having a private practice in psychotherapy. Eight years after I began my career, I was approached by my division chair at the college about teaching courses in the history of the Old and New Testaments, since a number of students were requesting them. He selected me to teach these religion courses because, he said, I was the only one on the faculty who had training and education in the Bible. For the next twenty-three years, I had the privilege of teaching the Bible in a secular institution! That opportunity came only because God had prepared me years before.

It's clear that God's call can mean different things. That's why it's useful, particularly for young pastors questioning the results of their ministry, to seek a deeper understanding of this call in light of their profile of strengths and weaknesses. In this matter, Christian professionals can be quite helpful, both in helping them to work through the emotional fallout of their disheartening experiences and in determining what God has best gifted them to do.

KNOWING YOUR GOALS

It may seem surprising that so many pastors are unclear about their specific goals beyond the broad generalization

31

of "preaching the Word." Other than spiritual growth, some have difficulty articulating the behavioral outcomes they're looking for. But it is important to have specific outcomes in mind in terms of attitudes, values, and behaviors that will be facilitated by the teaching of the Word and the administration of the church. Many pastors I've counseled have become quite discouraged by how little their congregations remember of their sermons, let alone how minimally they internalize the lessons. They wonder out loud whether they're doing anything useful at all.

The outcomes that are sought must carry intrinsic relevance to the hearers' concerns and struggles. If not, the message will simply be tuned out, or perhaps, crowded out by the more dramatic claims of life in the trenches. When you consider how many believers are, for whatever reasons, struggling quietly with depression, it's not surprising that sermons often fall on deaf ears. Nonetheless, one pastor said to me that he didn't address emotional issues like that because he believed that the church was called to address strictly spiritual issues. He apparently didn't think that emotional and spiritual issues comingled, unless, of course, sin was involved.

The point is that you can't approach strategic planning in your ministry effectively based on generic assumptions. If you want to work toward certain outcomes, you must first freely admit to what you don't know and then be open to what you discover in your own investigation. It's best when your goals represent the collective desires to know Scripture, to be sensitive to the leading of the Holy Spirit, and to truly connect with the needs of your congregation. (We will discuss this at greater length in a later chapter.) Suffice it to say, it is wise to have a carefully considered rationale for every step you take in your ministry. While the church is a place for hope, it is also a platform for thoughtful action.

NOTE

1. Kenneth Blanchard, interview by Laura Ingraham, *The Laura Ingraham Show*, January 21, 2003.

3

THE IMPORTANCE
OF KNOWING GOD

It was forty years ago that J. I. Packer initially published his seminal work on the fundamental difference between knowing God and knowing about God. The first is experiential, involving predominantly the spiritual self, and the second is largely intellectual, involving mainly the cognitive self. The former means communion in the transforming presence of God, seeking to know him more fully and individually investing in his redemptive love. The latter means studying the nature of God and his actions as a theological matter, to flesh out one's knowledge as a person of religion. It's the difference between humbly submitting to divine grace and seeking knowledge for its own sake. In other words, it's the difference between faith and religiosity.

We always have to be on the lookout for those subtle forms of conceit that can strip us of our humility. Pursuing theological knowledge has a lofty ring to it. But as Packer notes, there is always the danger that "the very greatness of the subject matter will intoxicate us and we shall come to think of ourselves as a cut above other Christians because of our interest in it and grasp of it."[1] No one, not even the pastor, is immune to this trap.

To be sure, personal discipline is important. It's imperative to first understand the attributes of the God we serve, to know the meaning of his words and actions as described in the Testaments (Old and New). To do this you must follow accepted hermeneutical principles, conduct sound exegesis, and carefully exposit the Scriptures. These things are at the heart of a pastor's diligence in biblical study. Such diligence takes a great deal of time and energy, but it's necessary to develop sermons that express fidelity to the Word. But acquiring knowledge does not constitute the only preparation pastors must do to keep their own spiritual life vital and congregations growing.

MAINTAINING THE PURITY OF FAITH

Without paying attention to the crucial task of knowing God, our theology can quickly descend into heterodoxy. The church can easily lapse into the postmodern idea of love apart from expectations, a concept far removed from the nature and character of God's love. J. I. Packer astutely observed that the "ignorance of God—ignorance both of his ways and of the practice of communion with him—lies at the root of much of the church's weakness today. . . . The irony is that modern Christians, preoccupied with maintaining religious practices in an irreligious world, have themselves allowed God to become remote."[2]

Studying about God's attributes as well as his words and actions is not the same as actually purposing to experience them. Study alone, though eye-opening and humbling, is not enough to nurture your spiritual life as a pastor. What you also need is time spent quietly reveling in the presence of God, allowing yourself to soak in the very love and divine holiness about which you preach. This is a time meant to be rich in prayer and meditation, evoking the deeper kind of spiritual renewal.

In contemplating God, the sum of our thoughts is like the smallest particle in the galaxies of the heavens. Just realizing the strain it takes to see the microscopic piece of knowledge we call "our understanding" brings us humbly to our knees in wonder over the immensity of God's glorious being. Who can fathom it? When finitude meets infinity, it inexorably produces awe, reverential fear, and transformation. It is in our awareness of our smallness and weakness that we are most likely to invite the greatness of God.

In these interludes of reflection, we are called to be still and know that God, in his eternal nature, never stops reaching out to fellowship with his own. It is part of his nature and character to bridge the chasm between the holy and unholy, to offer his righteousness as the only solution to our unrighteousness. To be humbled by this invitation means to realize we're usually not where we think we are before God. C. S. Lewis noted that "we easily imagine conditions far higher than any we've really reached. If we describe what we have imagined we make others, and make ourselves, believe that we have really been there."[3]

FINDING PEACE OF MIND
IN A CHAOTIC WORLD

Pastors must continuously bear in mind who they are and who God is and to know the vast difference between the two. I say this because you can become so comfortable in the daily routine of church activities that you become self-deceptively nonchalant in your spiritual life. There is always the danger that a pastor's life with God can become more a professional one than a moment-by-moment one. In other words, a religious one more than a spiritual one. It's in that moment that the impulse of intellectualized faith begins to morph into either a kind of nominalism or a kind of legalism that saps the very vitality that a life in God promises.

However, it is also easy to be swept up into the troubles of church administration so that you lose perspective and decry your call to the ministry. The majority of pastors have considered resignation from the ministry altogether at least once during their careers, and many who stay are chronically depressed. People don't enter the pastorate because they think it's a simple job. To the contrary, if they've taken church polity classes in seminary, they already know that it can be an incredibly complex and delicate operation. They know too that, without God's help, they're likely to falter. As anyone in the ministry can attest, church business can at times be very messy.

As a pastor, you know that many things compete for your attention. The needs of the people seem endless; the demands of the board require thought and circumspection . . . and usually timely action. Crises of one sort or another are not uncommon. Conflicts in the church often disrupt the rhythms of the calendar, sometimes requiring wearisome meetings that drag on into the night. Of course, the assistant is always there to remind you of forgotten appointments or the press of weekly responsibilities. And the list goes on. You know the routine. You can almost hear the guilt-laden protest rising from your throat that it's too much, that it's unrealistic to think that there is sufficient time to stand still long enough to luxuriate in the quiet presence of God.

Yet despite these realities, your spiritual nurture is not optional if you want your ministry to remain spiritually viable and emotionally stable. While this observation may not come as a surprise to you, it's nonetheless difficult to always heed the principle. Spiritual vitality has a way of slowly fading rather than suddenly disappearing. If it vanished quickly, it would more likely arouse your attention. Instead, your spiritual awareness can be imperceptibly compromised by the fact that you are, after all, caught up in "doing God's work" every day.

A BULWARK AGAINST DEPRESSION

I discussed earlier that depression can be a signal that something has gone awry in your relational world. This can very well also include your spiritual relationship with God. If nothing else, it can tell you that you have become organically disconnected from what gives you true meaning. It may call for a return to the apostle Paul's admonition to continually remind yourself of what is true, honorable, just, and worthy of praise— in other words, the larger picture of God's presence and the reason anything good exists in the first place (Phil. 4:8).

In this respect, there is some value in keeping a "gratitude log" in which you record every day at least three things you're grateful for, regardless of what else is going on. This simple exercise has proven to be a surprisingly powerful tool in coping with severe stress. In the military, they have found that when the troops are required to keep something akin to gratitude logs they are more resistant to the ravages of PTSD (post-traumatic stress disorder) following their return from the battlefield. This is most likely due to the fact that recalling things you're grateful for, even in the midst of traumatic events, provides the perspective to give needed balance to what's happening at the moment.

For a pastor, the spiritual implications of keeping perspective in daily ministry are of profound importance. It can make the difference between burnout and keeping your heart and mind intact during the turbulence that naturally occurs in the course of church life. Of even greater significance, however, is that such perspective, at least in spiritual terms, rightly upholds a pastor's confidence in the final justice of God's sovereign will. This knowledge of God's nature and character, in turn, invariably breeds peace, despite circumstances that are not always favorable.

Notice that the apostle Paul said he *learned* to be content (Phil. 4:11). It did not come to him naturally. As an intense protagonist of the gospel, he was emotionally volatile in his early history as a believer. But as his ministry progressed, he became calmer, and toward the end, even more diplomatic, explicitly giving his protégé, Timothy, instructions on how to properly handle easily offended members in the church (see, for example, 1 Tim. 5:1–2).

Seeking to know God, not merely to know about him, provides both a plumb line for doctrinal orthodoxy and a stimulus for more stable living. The pastor who makes this aim first priority centers the church in the desires of God's heart. Just as it was Paul's lesson on ways to handle anxiety, reminding yourself of the truth is, at once, the powerful corrective to the lies of postmodernism and the unsettling distress of a challenging ministry.

In the end, it's what defines the relationship between truth and freedom.

NOTES

1. J. I. Packer, *Knowing God* (London: Hodder & Stoughton, 1973), 5.

2. Ibid., 1, foreword.

3. C. S. Lewis, *The Four Loves* (New York: Harcourt, 1960), 140.

4

THE IMPORTANCE OF KNOWING YOUR LIMITS

Many books have been written about the importance of setting personal boundaries in order to live a life that's marked by both responsibility and freedom. Such boundaries are limits that you create to define reasonable and acceptable ways in which you want other people to respond to you. They define you as an individual who takes ownership of your thoughts, opinions, and actions, and who is proactive about making them known to others when circumstances call for it. In short, it is a summons to live assertively.

Assertiveness is the cornerstone of intimacy. God has invited us into an assertive relationship with him precisely because he wants a kinship of the intimate kind. His love asks for an honest response of faith, not the dishonest dance of fear. In relationships, assertive living generally means respecting others as well as yourself. It means open self-disclosure while accepting the give-and-take of requests for change. This stands in stark contrast with passivity, which ultimately means disrespecting yourself, and aggression, which invariably means disrespecting the other person. Passive people are marked by the self-rejecting silence of withdrawal, while aggressive people are characterized by the self-projecting bluster of coercion. Passive people recoil; aggressive people retaliate; and assertive people reach out and cooperate. Passivity is based on fear, aggression on self-importance, and assertiveness on the desire for humble engagement.

Setting boundaries is, then, an assertive act of respecting self and others. It protects you from exceeding your limits while protecting others from the temptation to sinfully exploit the relationship. It invites creative conflict resolution and discourages emotional manipulation. And it makes more likely a union of mutual regard. This suggests that setting boundaries is godly behavior, deserving the attention of every believer who wishes to serve the Lord well.

THE CHALLENGE OF BOUNDARIES

Why is it difficult for so many people, especially Christians, to establish boundaries? To answer this question, we often do not need to look any further than a personal history of guilt-inducing interactions. Whether by family patterns of manipulation or by church-inspired legalism, many come to believe that unless they comply with the demands of others they are rebellious, bad, or sinful. As a result, the fear of disapproval becomes a form of tyranny. They will do almost anything to avoid it, sacrificing their needs, desires, and opinions without hesitation. Conformity to what others think is, to the people-pleaser, the royal highway to tranquility. As Christians, they frequently misconstrue service to others to mean doing whatever others ask.

Obedience to this standard becomes the rationale used to justify passivity, to suggest that saying no is tantamount to a refusal to serve the Christian community. It doesn't matter if they are already burdened with other responsibilities— they simply think that they are required by love to always say yes. One author summed up this kind of boundary-less living with a book entitled *When I Say No, I Feel Guilty.* Such guilt is a trap that imprisons its victims in an inflexible maze of strict rules that leave little room for wise judgment.

When pastors suffer from the inability to set appropriate boundaries, the stress of working with so many others who make demands on their time can be overwhelming. Perhaps, that's why so many pastors work an exhausting sixty-hour week. Especially when the church is relatively small and the numbers of staff are few, the tendency to be the jack-of-all-trades becomes almost irresistible. But even in large churches where there are many staff members to handle the load, the demands are exponentially greater and the number of concepts for various programs only proliferates.

One pastor developed the wise strategy of encouraging people with a new idea for ministry to take the initiative to flesh out the proposal themselves. If they're still sold on it after that, then they are asked to bring it to the board for approval as a ministry they're willing to head. That way the pastor is not personally in charge of implementing every creative and exciting idea for ministry. Instead, it becomes a shared vision with members of the congregation. The success of this boundary-setting strategy is seen not only in the way it frees the pastor, but also in the manner it encourages a more proactive church.

If you fail to protect yourself like this because you're trying so hard to please everyone, eventually physical and emotional exhaustion will be the result. This was the plight of Moses, complicated still further by the fact that he was in charge of an entire nation. He had great difficulty delegating responsibility, feeling obligated to take on every task himself. If the people demanded something, he complied, though they were rarely satisfied. Even his father-in-law saw the emotional crash coming if he didn't change course. The problem is that you often don't see it yourself until you're already physically and emotionally spent.

People-pleasing is a painful experience, especially when those whom you serve are unappreciative of what you do. But even if they give you approval, it can become still worse if they merely keep piling on more demands. Just as God instructed Moses that it was a good thing to set boundaries, so he instructs pastors today who struggle with the same problem. He has no desire for his servants to wear themselves out trying to do the impossible. He knows that nothing but depression awaits if they do.

THE EXAMPLE FOR THE AGES

Notice how Jesus handled this issue in his earthly ministry. People were constantly demanding more of his time. They wanted more healing, more preaching and teaching. They simply could not get enough. Everywhere he went, throngs pressed in upon him. Questions were shouted at him. Pleas of desperation were directed toward him. Constant criticisms were hurled his way. No matter what he did, there was some group aggrieved by his words or deeds. This was not a situation for the fainthearted and certainly not for the emotional survival of a people pleaser. But Jesus was not enslaved by the need for social approval. He recognized in advance the importance of periodic rest, which is why he appropriately resisted when urged by the people to keep ministering beyond the point of exhaustion.

Often he went up into the mountains, a favorite retreat of his, either to be alone or to fellowship with his disciples. On one occasion, he left the crowds and climbed aboard the disciples' boat, promptly falling into a deep sleep. His need for rest was self-evident. By example, he was demonstrating to his servants how important it was to pace themselves in their ministry or otherwise they would not last.

These sidebars about periodic trips to the mountains or the sea were included in the biblical record, I think, to provide a template for all those down through the ages who have undertaken the ministry of the gospel. Understanding your limits is pivotal to your mental and physical health. Not all pastors can handle the same load, nor can the same load be handled by the pastor all the time.

THE IMPORTANCE OF REVIEWING LIMITS

Virtually everyone experiences highs and lows in life. This is certainly *not* something for which to feel guilty or inadequate. Rather it means that it's useful to periodically review where you are in your energy levels and emotional stamina to determine whether some kind of change would be helpful. There can be many reasons, including medical ones, which could account for difficulties you may encounter.

It's also important to know your limits in terms of what is reasonable in light of the needs of your family. Too many marriages and too many children have been unwittingly sacrificed because the demands of ministry have superseded the importance of a pastor's personal life.

After reviewing everything that's on your plate, you may determine that it's wise to turn down that further request for help or that invitation to become involved in an additional ministry. Others might object, but you are doing the right thing. Setting your boundaries so as not to exceed your limits is not only in your best interest, but also in the best interests of others. When you begin to waver in your defense of those boundaries, remember the example you've been given. Like Jesus before you, you will then have mastered the idea of properly allotting to yourself the time you need for adequate renewal. In so doing, you may very well have preserved your sanity . . . and your ministry.

5

KNOWING WHEN
YOU ARE DEPRESSED

Though depression is common among pastors, they are sometimes the last ones to recognize it or, at least, openly admit to it. Part of the problem is that no one expects pastors to be struggling with depression. Instead, they think that, because their walk with God is so strong, pastors will always find refuge in their faith, as if pastors always live above the fray. Yet ironically, congregation members are often relieved and find pastors more approachable when they discover they wrestle with similar issues.

With such misconceptions about faith and depression, no one can blame pastors for trying to hide being burdened with emotional pain. They usually have willing accomplices to help keep the secret too. That's why the usual routine can often last a remarkable length of time. Unless the depression lifts on its own, however, it cannot remain a secret forever. Often a medical professional is the one who finally makes the diagnosis of depression.

THE EMOTIONAL CONSEQUENCES OF DOING NOTHING

Until a diagnosis of depression, the pastor may simply have explained away dark feelings as "burnout," a term that carries with it fewer negative connotations. It suggests, instead, that a busy schedule is making the pastor tired and what is required is some rest. There may, of course, be some truth to that. But it may also be that the pastor (and congregation) is willing to accept almost any explanation short of calling it what it is.

However, like many in the congregation, it's more likely that the pastor simply fails to understand the reality of being depressed. Many people have difficulty recognizing when they are experiencing depression. Rather, they have an amazing capacity to adapt to a life in which they are resigned to feeling down. They may believe that's just the way life is. Only when their negative mood greatly intensifies, perhaps to the point of suicidal ideation, do they become alarmed enough to seek some kind of help. Sadly, many of them don't do so even then.

Because pastors are on the front line of dealing with others who are hurting in some way, they carry a special burden as caregivers. Rarely are they extensively trained in counseling, but they nonetheless are called upon to make fairly sophisticated assessments of people seeking their help. The weight of this responsibility alone can trigger anxiety and depression, particularly in pastors who feel at a loss of what to do and fear doing the wrong thing. One pastor I knew counseled a deeply troubled young man who ended up committing suicide. He was so devastated by this result that he subsequently resigned from the pastorate to work at a parachurch organization committed solely to evangelization. The trauma of this event was merely the disastrous endpoint to his deep ambivalence about counseling in the first place.

The irony is that, sometimes, pastors, like those they counsel, can't see the severity of the problems brewing in themselves. Instead, they may only vaguely sense they're not in a good place. In fact, I've counseled a few pastors who have nervously admitted to me that they're pretty much winging it whenever they wander beyond spiritual matters. The fact is that they are humans first and thus share the same tendencies to have blind spots as anyone else.

If what I have described sounds familiar, you know it would be immensely helpful to quickly recognize the characteristics of depression when you see them. You would then be able to determine in a timely fashion if a person needs to seek professional help. Equally important, armed with knowledge of the specific symptoms, you're also in a better position to identify them in yourself.

THE CHARACTERISTICS OF DEPRESSION

The following is a list of common symptoms typical of depression that can help you identify which and how many you are experiencing:

- Feelings of sadness and emptiness
- Feelings of helplessness and hopelessness
- Loss of interest or pleasure in life activities
- Loss of energy or constant fatigue
- Insomnia (difficulty getting to sleep or staying asleep)
- Feelings of intense anxiety
- Changes in appetite and weight
- Excessive or misplaced guilt
- Feelings of worthlessness
- Physical symptoms such as bodily aches and pains
- Sometimes increased agitation, including outbursts of anger and irritability
- Difficulties thinking and concentrating
- Recurrent thoughts of death or suicide

It's important to know that you don't need to have all of the described symptoms at once to be diagnosed as depressed. All you need is four or more of them to confirm the diagnosis. While some symptoms are more common than others, you should carefully review each one before determining whether you are suffering from depression. For evidence of the level of this depression, you can take the Hamilton Survey for Physical and Emotional Wellness available at www.depressionoutreach.com.

KNOWING THE MAIN TYPES OF DEPRESSION

When your symptoms of depression are disabling, where even routine tasks seem impossible, and this lasts for at least two consecutive weeks, you're probably suffering a *major depressive episode*. It's with these episodes that suicidal thoughts (and attempts) are most likely. However, if such symptoms, in much less severe form, endure chronically for at least two years, you're more likely experiencing what we call *dysthymia*. If you are dysthymic, you're likely to continue with your responsibilities despite persistent unhappiness and hopelessness.

Though it's not wise, most people with dysthymic disorder often slug it out with life on their own, rather than seeking professional help. Even though they're despondent, they are usually not in danger of hospitalization. Instead, they often rely on close friends or family, or maybe a compassionate colleague, to help them through. With pastors, it's usually family and close staff members, especially assistants upon whom they rely to run interference for them. When they do come in for counseling, they usually must deal with their sense of failure first before they are ready to take on the work of sorting through their issues.

There are some pastors who wrestle with *bipolar disorder*, a spectrum disorder in which symptoms swing from mania to deep depression. This affects about six million adults or about 2.5 percent of the population. In the manic phase, they may be marked by excessive euphoria or excitement, racing thoughts, sudden changes from being happy or joyful to being irritable or angry, restlessness, high energy and racing thoughts along with rapid talking, little need for sleep, making grandiose and unattainable plans to the point of being delusional, and impulsivity (such as spending sprees, increased and/or inappropriate sexual activity, alcohol abuse, or reckless ventures). These symptoms can vary in intensity, the milder form often referred to as hypomania. When they emotionally swing the other way, they can enter into a very deep depression, greatly increasing the risk of suicide. This disorder is about 80 percent biological and about 20 percent environmentally triggered, which strongly suggests the need for both medication and counseling.

For pastors, bipolar disorder is particularly troubling, since most of these behaviors are categorically opposed to the life believers are called to live. Indeed, they can be potentially hospitalized or even jailed for some of their manic excesses. The good news is that proper medication can usually control the bipolar symptoms reasonably well and therapy can provide the strategies needed to stay out of harm's way.

As the long list of symptoms indicates, the characteristics of depression can vary considerably from person to person. However, its expression is not without a pattern. Generally speaking, depression is most often expressed behaviorally in any one of five individual syndromes. First, there are the *withdrawn depressives*, who, while feeling worthless and helpless and having lost interest and energy to do anything, are especially characterized by apathy and a kind of "what's the use?" quality to their thinking. They are the type who sit for hours alone with the doors and windows shut, withdrawn and lifeless. They do everything they can to avoid people.

Then there are the *dependent depressives*, who, in addition to the usual symptoms, develop a clinging dependency on others, draining them dry by making constant demands. They do this because they feel overwhelmingly helpless inside. In contrast to the withdrawn depressives, dependent depressives endlessly seek out people.

Third, there are the *somatic depressives*, who express their troubled emotions through persistent bodily complaints of one kind or another. These hypochondriacs are really depressed people in a constant, usually unsuccessful, search for personal significance.

Fourth, there are the *angry depressives*, who express their despair in sometimes intense anger at others or themselves. They are the ultimate pessimists, with deep guilt and blame thrown in. Since they're not easy to live with, their marriages are often in very poor shape as well.

Finally, there are the *anxiety depressives*, who are constantly worrying, creating worst-case scenarios about almost every circumstance. They often suffer from acute anxiety attacks, during which they suffer heart palpitations, feelings that they're going to faint, tightening in their chest (and other muscles), and difficulty breathing. Because of these symptoms, it's hardly surprising to find them in the emergency room, thinking they're having a heart attack. It's important to know that anxiety is frequently a precursor to depression, as well as a common component of it. Those who suffer these symptoms feel like they are constantly waiting for "the other shoe to drop." Needless to say, they live in a depressing world dominated by persistent feelings of dread.

You no doubt have seen these syndromes many times in troubled church members you have counseled. You may even see one of these patterns in yourself. The important thing is to recognize the symptoms as early as possible so that you can take appropriate action to make a difference.

ACCEPTING THE NEED FOR HELP

Whether pastors seek help or not depends, at least in part, upon their view of counseling. If they see it as unnecessary because they must work their problems out spiritually and therapists are not trained to do that, or if they believe psychology is hostile to spiritual things, they're unlikely to seek professional guidance. If they consider psychologists, even Christian ones, as unwitting tools of the Devil or hucksters who overcharge for their work, again they will recoil from therapy. Only if they understand therapy as a useful means of uncovering the source of despair, and don't consider it a challenge to faith, will they be amenable to the idea of counseling. Even then, it can be difficult if they think of themselves as having disappointed God. In fact, because of this, they may very well become depressed about their depression, which only makes things worse.

As a therapist, I'm quite familiar with these points of view. I've heard them from the pulpit, encountered them among some of my clients, and read books and articles questioning the value of psychological insight. I wrote an article for a publication to pastors and church leaders recently, and it was welcomed by those who see the usefulness of Christian professional counseling. But it also received negative feedback from some who are ill-disposed toward all things psychological. I accept that there are different opinions on these matters and invite honest dialogue about them.

Nonetheless, I grieve the fact that there are many pastors who, even though they know they're depressed, languish in their emotional pain, confused about why, as servants of God, they have fallen victim to emotional collapse. They may even feel abandoned by God. Like many of the prophets and kings of old, they cry out, "My God, my God, why have you forsaken me?" (Ps. 22:1). Or as Elijah put it, "Take my life; I am no better than my ancestors" (1 Kings 19:4).

I am convinced that God does not want our self-condemnation, but rather our acknowledgement of his mercy and compassion. Depression is our compass in finding new direction to our lives, our wake-up call to address problems or previous wounds that are holding us back from realizing the full potential of God's handiwork in us. The first step is accepting depression, not as a sign of spiritual weakness, but as an alarm telling us of the need for growth or change in some area of our lives. Because it profoundly affects our relationship with God, it is his desire to be a part of the solution. Seeking professional help or being prescribed medication does not change that.

6

DEVELOPING FRIENDSHIPS
OUTSIDE THE CHURCH

One of the most common reasons people are dissatisfied with their church is the lack of meaningful relationships within the body. In other words, they're lonely, suffering from a lack of attachment. In a similar manner, one of the reasons pastors are dissatisfied with their lives as leaders of the church is the lack of meaningful relationships outside their congregations. They too are yearning for friendship.

THE CONSEQUENCES OF ISOLATION

It may seem surprising to learn how little a pastor fellowships with other pastors in the community, other than a phone call now and then. Indeed, studies show that the overwhelming majority of pastors do not have any close friends, and therefore, no one in whom to confide their troubles. The truth is churches rarely share facilities or activities, let alone interact on a personal level. This isolation tends to shed some light on the problem of a pastor's loneliness in a crowd. There is already a built-in obstacle to developing close relationships or confidants in their own congregations, especially since it automatically involves a dual role. For instance, they can hardly air grievances about their work with someone who is also a church member.

One pastor told me that he made the mistake of speaking confidentially with the head elder in the church about his feelings toward a rather defiant member, and it soon leaked out, causing an unpleasant backlash from friends of the other man. He said he quickly realized that he could not be that open with someone in the church, particularly if he or she were in leadership. He felt that his wife was the only one he was comfortable sharing things with and, even then, he was afraid some issues would be too stressful for her. He longed for someone with whom he could speak freely without always second-guessing whether it was alright to do so.

WHAT DOES FRIENDSHIP MEAN?

C. S. Lewis once observed that "friendship is unnecessary, like philosophy, like art. . . . It has no survival value; rather it is one of those things which give value to survival."[1] Companionship is what makes life on earth more worth living. It's God's social contract with us to offer fellowship with him so that we might discover a friendship that promises change from the inside out. He knows that freely presenting who we are is our gift to him, just as crafting who we can become is his gift to us. It's a gift forged out of the bonds of a new family—new brothers and sisters—born from the same spiritual womb. You know what I mean when you step into a new group of believers, introducing yourself to people you've never met before, and immediately sense a kinship, a connection that far transcends any logical explanation.

As a pastor, this means finding a shared experience anywhere God is honored beyond the walls of your church. It's of consequence that you seek friendship outside your congregation because you can greatly profit from relationships that do not carry the expectations of leadership. Friendship with peers is freeing since there are no roles other than what you make of them. Outside companions can also provide another, more objective source of feedback to your thoughts and ideas of action. In this way, you can test the wisdom of your thinking in the arena of fresh perspectives unfastened to the patterns of your church. More importantly, however, you have the chance to truly relax in the unconditional embrace of those who care for you as a trusted friend, not as a pastor who needs the relationships of allies.

Breathing in the fresh air of a circle of associates (including other ministers) who are unconnected to one's church provides the pastor with the emotional renewal necessary for the trials sure to come. It's not that good friendships within the church are not richly beneficial. It's just that outside relationships generally do not carry the baggage of church business. In difficult times, especially, we all find strength in empathy. Empathy is feeling *with* a person, as opposed to sympathy, which is feeling *for* a person. Few people realize just how much empathic encouragement a well-meaning pastor needs when an agitated member of the congregation destroys (or at least tries to destroy) the good will of long, hard efforts to forge a consensus. It doesn't take many disgruntled people to turn things upside down by creating unforeseen conflicts that puzzle and subsequently incense the less informed.

I counseled a pastor who had tried to help a woman in his church seemingly going through a rough patch in her life. But she had suddenly turned on him and accused him of inappropriate behavior. Stunned by the accusations, he spent the next several months defending himself in numerous meetings with the board.

It was later discovered that this was not the first time this woman had falsely accused someone of wrongdoing in a church. In fact, she had a history of displaying behaviors characteristic of borderline personality disorder. The pastor, of course, was naïve about this sort of thing and thus was completely unprepared for the boomerang effect of trying to help someone he didn't know very well. Though eventually cleared of any malfeasance, this pastor afterward became very depressed. Having no one to turn to, he was left to his own ruminations of failure. He was convinced that his ministry at the church, which previously had been quite successful, was now permanently compromised. He felt that everything he had worked for in his congregation had been dealt a death blow. "How will it be any different anywhere else I go?" he asked. "From now on, I'm going to be very reticent to reach out to others. I think I'll just stick to preaching."

This wounded pastor was a casualty of inexperience with pathologically manipulative people. Sometimes, friendships with others outside the church who are savvy to the ways of the mentally disordered can make a world of difference in understanding their potential for wreaking havoc in the congregation. One thing is certain: There will always be people who arrive at the doorstep of the church with the persuasive veneer of spirituality, but who are the embodiment of trouble waiting to happen.

NAVIGATING ISSUES FROM THE OUTSIDE IN

Behavioral pathology can, of course, take many forms, some of which can escape notice simply because they are so commonplace. Gossip, for example, has always been a problem in the church, even though it is often dismissed as a "lesser sin" by those obsessed with the higher profile indiscretions of greater public impact. Rumors can pinwheel across the social landscape of the church now more rapidly than ever before, thanks to cell phones, Facebook, and Twitter. Truth and fiction are constantly dueling for adherents, leading to misunderstanding, dysfunction, and prejudice. Minor differences explode into major divisions, and suspicions grow into accusations.

Friendships external to the congregation can enable you to view what's happening differently than when you're too close to the situation to grasp events accurately. Just as outside mediation groups are sometimes called in to evaluate church conflict, so too can ongoing relationships with other pastors provide a way for you to reassess problems and do something about them before they metastasize to the entire congregation. The principle is always the same: The earlier you recognize and address spiritually and emotionally unhealthy practices in the church, the more likely you'll be successful in restoring the body. If certain friendships can significantly help you in these matters, so much the better.

Some pastors broaden their base of contacts to purposely include unbelievers who challenge them to see life through secular, even atheistic or agnostic eyes. It sharpens their minds to address, for instance, social issues that attract diverse groups of activists or to confront common issues of religious belief that dispute basic principles of Christian doctrine. Author and pastor Tim Keller's interactions with young, largely skeptical urban professionals in New York are an example of this kind of outreach. They are drawn to his willingness to confront the hard issues, the ones that generate the greatest criticisms from those in their group. They also admire his authenticity and openness to really listen to them. From these interactions have come some of Dr. Keller's most significant theological discussions for those questioning God's relevance.

Years ago I was asked by a local seminary professor, whom I knew, to come to one of his classes on hermeneutics and present myself as an atheist. He had a hunch that many of these pastors-in-training, though students of the Word, didn't really know how to develop a persuasive argument against atheism. As a Christian who was acquainted with the various philosophical points of view and who was, as well, a professor of religion and psychology at a secular college, I knew the arguments on both sides of the aisle.

After presenting the case for atheism, I opened it up for questions and answers. Students became visibly upset when every challenge they made to what I said was turned on its head. After the class ended, without revealing my true identity,

I left. The next day, this professor called and told me that it was one of the most profitable sessions his class had ever had. His students had been humbled by the realization that they didn't know as much as they thought they did. He reported that they returned to their studies with keener minds, determined to be better prepared.

This is what sometimes happens when we rub shoulders with those who are opposed to our Christian views. Not only do we become better acquainted with the secular mind-set, but we develop a sharper message for others to consider. Jesus spent much of his ministry eating and interacting with sinners. Indeed, he was roundly criticized by the self-righteous Pharisees for doing so (Matt. 9:10–13). But he knew how to make the greatest impact on his listeners.

THE STIMULUS FACTOR

When you, as a pastor, decide to befriend others who differ widely from your views, it introduces a certain level of authenticity. What's more, you'll often be gratified by the welcome you receive. Remember, there is always the danger of otherwise becoming insular in your ways when you limit your relationships to members of the church. When this is the case, you fail to fully appreciate the stimulation unbelievers can have on your thinking. You can count on people who do not follow Jesus to bring a very different perspective, one which your congregants are exposed to almost every day in their place of work, school, or community.

This can be an incentive to frame your sermons in terms that better equip your flock to communicate their faith to a world unsympathetic to their beliefs. This is particularly important to those forced to confront the sometimes hostile challenges of others. Like the seminary students described above, many of the Christians I taught in college were completely unprepared to adequately defend their faith in the face of opposition from unbelieving professors. This is one area in which the church can usefully expand its ministry. We can't assume that because Christians go to church regularly, they automatically understand how to deal effectively with such challenges.

Not only can expanding your circle of associates to include those outside the church help you guard against depression, it can also invigorate your ministry in some of the most powerful and consequential ways.

NOTE

1. C. S. Lewis, *The Four Loves* (New York: Harcourt, 1960), 71.

7

DEVELOPING SUPPORTIVE RELATIONSHIPS INSIDE THE CHURCH

For pastors, church is their workplace, and their colleagues are members of the church. In other words, work and fellowship, business and worship are comingled. Pastors find their career aspirations, spiritual fulfillment, and relational sustenance mostly in one place. You find them there during the week, and they are still there on the weekends. In fact, their busiest days are on the weekends. Outside of home, they are "on" most of the time. In many respects, this pastoral bubble extends to the pastor's family as well. In all of these ways, the pastor's situation is unique . . . and packed with pressure.

How does a minister maximize satisfaction and effectiveness in serving the needs of a congregation? How can you avoid the common pitfalls of pastoring a church? What can you do to minimize the exhaustion of an around-the-clock shepherd? The answers to these questions usually, for the most part, determine your staying power in the pulpit.

KNOWING THE DISTRIBUTION OF POWER IN YOUR CHURCH

When I was in seminary, a veteran pastor of a large church in Southern California taught my church polity class. Perhaps the most significant point he made that term was his comment on power relationships within the church. He argued that the first priority of every pastor who is new to a congregation is to determine which people or groups of people wield the real influence in decision-making for the body.

As this professor rightly pointed out, you must know the configuration and distribution of power among members of the church in order to effectively administer the plans you have as pastor. Sometimes, long-term members or founding families wield great power, and if you don't consult them before you make a decision, you'll likely experience considerable pushback.

This happened to one young pastor I counseled who had taken a pastorate in an old, relatively rural church whose congregation had remained small for many decades. This pastor had virtually a cornucopia of exciting new ideas to implement in this church, ideas which held the promise of significant growth. But when he started his pastorate, he made the mistake of convening the elder board and informing them of his plans, naïvely expecting them to be excited about them too. Within a year of his arrival, the heavy-weights of the board, whose authority seemed threatened, unceremoniously asked him to resign. Confused and devastated, this budding pastor decided to give up the ministry because, as he put it, "So many Christians are just too rigid." What he didn't realize was that those in long-time positions of unquestioned power come to believe that the will of the congregation is always the same as theirs. It was important to consult them first, to give them time to "own" the ideas for themselves, before he made any grand announcements.

This highlights the reason why some of the best-laid plans are aborted before they ever see the light of day. I was once on a church education committee in which it was actually said by a committee member that the new plan we were considering shouldn't be tried, principally because it had never been done before. As this common response demonstrates, the resistance to novel thinking is not necessarily logical.

Besides the powerful members of the congregation, there can also be dissension within the pastoral staff. There are various reasons why staff members might object to a policy in the church. But the manner of dealing with the conflict often reveals the staff members' level of transparency. If staff members come to you directly to discuss the issue, they are probably sincere in their efforts to present their ideas without prejudice. However, if their opposition goes behind your back, then it inevitably becomes a problem for the entire body. This is where your proactive leadership is especially important—not the threatened, dictatorial kind that implies "it's my way or the highway," but rather the examining, interactive kind that makes resolution a priority for the sake of the church. Remember, a timely response can prevent differences from becoming destructively schismatic. It can also quietly forestall another potential source of depression.

Every pastor would benefit, then, by rethinking how to introduce plans and directives, especially to those who might already be wary, to buy the time necessary for properly preparing the ground for new ideas. This might involve thoughtful inquiry into others' thinking in order to provoke their internal reassessment of old ways of doing things. When you eventually arrive at the destination of your intentions, they will be much more likely to be on board, because they feel they've been heard. They may perhaps even think your ideas are fundamentally the same as theirs, in which case a bond of common thinking between you is formed.

WHY PEOPLE SEEK POSITIONS OF POWER

As an essentially voluntary association, the church is subject to many of the same social dynamics as are other, more politically organized groups. Some people want to feel important, to feel that what they do really matters to others, but aren't experiencing that in their lives. So they will tend to gravitate toward positions of power, wherever they can, to satisfy this desire. In the church, this may be cloaked in terms of spiritual service.

To be sure, many serve the church selflessly (and often tirelessly) out of conviction and dedication to our Lord. It's true also that solid believers who have natural leadership abilities, who often head their own departments or companies at work, are often wisely invited to use these skills in the church. Still, the opportunity to exert influence presents a strong attraction to others who cannot find it elsewhere and at times this can become a problem. Since there's power in adopted plans affecting the whole church, it is not too difficult to imagine that, on occasion, these people might raise objections simply because it was not originally their idea.

As one in the ministry, you may be rankled by the apparent pettiness of such infighting, but remember your first responsibility is to the flock you serve, and they are subject to the same frailties as is common to all of humanity. Just as God takes us where we are, not where we should be, so also must you as pastor take the people where they are before you can take them to where they can be. God will work his sovereign will in your midst, sometimes in spite of the church's failings. The apostle Paul put this point in perspective when he acknowledged the paradox that when we're weak, that's when we're strong. In other words, we're more likely to get out of the way and see God's hand at work when good things come from flawed people. That's because we can't attribute the success to our own strengths. You see, God has this great habit of displaying his creative power by snatching victory from the jaws of defeat. To God is the glory.

THE COMMON STRUGGLE WITH CHANGE

Another factor affecting social dynamics within the church is the general resistance of people to the prospect of anything new. Change—anything that deviates from what is familiar—represents varying degrees of threat to people who find their security in the status quo. I commonly encounter this phenomenon in the counseling room. Consequently, change must often be introduced incrementally in order to reduce fear and increase the likelihood of acceptance. It may seem considerably slower to do it this way, but in the long run it improves the chances that such change will be internalized. Those who refuse to concede this point but rather push ahead full steam will probably find rebellion on their hands. This is partly what happened to the young pastor I described above, though he didn't intend to alienate anyone by doing so.

Developing friendships in the church is an important ingredient in the recipe for a smooth transition to a different way of doing things. When such friends have been longtime members of the congregation, they can provide a window into the history of that body, knowledge that can be applied to the pastor's leadership of change. In this way, their presence represents continuity to the church and encouragement, maybe even boldness, for the pastor. Friendship can therefore serve as a vehicle not only for understanding how best to inaugurate change amongst a particular group of people, but also for a growing confidence to take prudent risk.

FRIENDSHIP AS AN ENDOWMENT

One pastor confided that developing a strong and respectful working relationship with the chairman of the board of deacons was one of the best investments he'd ever made. Their lasting friendship over the years is what sustained him during one of the darkest periods of his life, in which a severe bout with depression left him temporarily unable to lead the church. This friend faithfully filled the gap of leadership while the pastor recovered and was personally responsible for rallying the congregation in prayerful support for the success of his treatment. What's more, this friend visited him nearly every day. He was truly a heaven-sent Titus in this pastor's life. "I don't know if I would have made it without his constant companionship and reassurance during those cheerless days," he said as his voice trailed off in pensive reflection.

Just as God promised his sovereign help to quell the fears Moses had of reentering Egypt by providing Aaron, so also does he faithfully respond to the needs of his servants today. To this end, he has given us the capacity for friendship as an endowment. It is, as it were, a dowry of love.

When I think of the lyrics of the old hymn "What a Friend We Have in Jesus," I'm reminded of how important friendship is and how Christ himself fulfilled it. Certainly, he meant it to be no less important in our relationships with one another. This truth is especially meaningful in a society increasingly connected more by technology than by face-to-face interaction. Where texting is more common than eye contact, the presence of real people takes on even greater significance. Perhaps that's why the writer to the Hebrews reminds us not to forget the impact of assembling ourselves together. It's the lifeblood of sociability among believers.

8

KNOWING YOUR CONGREGATION

Many references have been made to the social dynamics and reactionary tendencies of congregations that the pastor must work with to make headway into their spiritual lives. In some ways, it's like a reality show in which the participants (like pastors and their staffs) are required to confront stiff challenges and avoid major blunders in order to emerge successful in the end. Or, at times, when there are agitators in their midst, it may seem more like the gladiator games of ancient Rome where the people gathered to witness the spectacle of warriors battling their adversaries. In either case, there are those who watch the struggles of the contestants with intense interest to see who will fail. These are the pessimists who give thumbs-down to almost everything others try to do. However, there are the partisan optimists who wildly cheer on their favorites to overcome all the odds. These are the ones who are not easily discouraged by the opposition.

DISPARATE GROUPS WITHIN THE CHURCH

It is sad to say that there are sometimes a disgruntled few in the congregation who take an almost perverse interest in the pastor's struggles. It may be that they have not received the same attention the previous pastor had given them—attention they think they deserve. Or else, they are people who are not happy with their own lives and do not abide very well those who are. They want to believe everyone is more or less in the same boat—a case of misery loves company. In any event, these are the ones who rapaciously feed the rumor mill and the gossip mongering crowd that are unfortunately found in almost every body of believers. Yet there are others who do everything in their power to assist or cheer on the pastor to maximize the pastor's chance of success in effectively shepherding the flock. Those warm encouragements at the door or that readiness to respond to every call for volunteers are examples of what these folks tend to do. It has been said that 80 percent of the work is done by 20 percent of the people. In many cases, that's not far from the truth.

In between these groups are the largely silent majority who are there because they enjoy the worship service or the fellowship, but who are, at best, only marginally interested or involved in anything else. These are people whose frantically busy lives and tangential interest in the full prerogatives of church membership keep them at a distance from greater participation. They are the ones you may see on Sunday mornings but rarely get to know beyond the ritual greetings before or after the services. Though they attend church regularly, they are also the first ones to leave when things are not going smoothly or there is trouble of some sort in the body.

These three groups—the intensely committed, the marginally involved, and the intrinsically disgruntled—represent the main challenges that face the pastor who attempts to lead this band of believers to a greater love of our Lord. The first group seeks spiritual growth, the second, fulfilled obligation, and the third, personal aggrandizement. One is motivated by strong convictions, another by a strong conscience, and the last by a strong desire for "justice." But all of them want their presence to matter.

Such differences exist because people check neither their personalities nor their personal lives at the door of the church. They bring both their most endearing strengths and their most troublesome weaknesses with them. Together, they contribute to the characteristic habits of the congregation. As pastor of this heterogeneous group, you must recognize the competing forces at work within your church and, rather than disparage them, build them into a cohesive body ready to serve God, like Jesus did with his disciples. This is a monumental task, one that makes your role unique and perilous.

It calls for both the exercise of God-given skill and the conscious cultivation of emotional strength. However, unless you rely on God's wisdom and power and on specific strategies that bring people together, you can expect rough seas ahead. And with the tossing waves comes the increased risk of the motion sickness called depression. Perhaps this stress, more than anything else, is what severely challenges the staying power of any minister of the gospel.

MAKING THE CHURCH RELEVANT WITHOUT COMPROMISING TRUTH

If you wanted to distill the entire Bible down to a few words, it would be that God is telling each one of us that we matter to him. So much so, that he gave his only Son, Jesus Christ, to die a timely death so that we might live a timeless life. We cannot earn such a life. It can only be given to us. This is the good news that must constantly resonate within the body, regardless of the reasons people are there. But tailoring this message to address the specific needs of the congregation is the real call of the pastor.

It's important to take the time and energy to carefully assess these needs, to know what they are and their value to you, and to communicate that value to those you serve. You would do well to inform them just how much this assessment will shape the nature of your ministry. This lets them know how serious you are in applying the Word of God to ways that relate to their pressing concerns. Remember, this is a social body, which means that for many, fellowshipping with friends is a key reason for their participation. Many years ago, my wife and I were members of a lively "young marrieds" class in the church, and they still hold well-attended reunions to this day. It was, for some, the main reason they stayed in that church.

Contributing to his powerful appeal to his listeners, Jesus deliberately shaped his message of redemption around the needs of those to whom he ministered. For example, to the Samaritan woman at the well, he addressed not only her marital situation, her promiscuous lifestyle, and the prejudices of her religious and social beliefs, but he also challenged the cultural taboo against Jews speaking directly to Samaritans. The woman was awed by the pinpoint accuracy of his analysis of her situation and consequently entranced by the power of his message of acceptance. Jesus understood the importance of getting her attention by addressing her thirst for a purpose-centered life.

In like manner, the best way for you to increase the relevance of your own sermons and, therefore, the likelihood that they will be internalized for personal change and spiritual growth is to speak directly into your congregants' lives. That means visiting with representative samples of your core constituency to understand what makes them tick and what really drives them. What do they feel is missing in their lives? How are the pivotal changes that our culture is undergoing affecting them? What do they worry about concerning their children? What family concerns are occupying their time and energy? What fears for their future do they have? How do they see God through their filters? How does their faith impact what they do or don't do, see or don't see? What stresses or crises are they currently facing? Does the life they're living make sense to them?

These are just a few of the questions you can ask in trying to understand the things that are on the minds of the people God has given you to serve. Touch upon these in your ministry, and you will most surely hit some nerves. Ignore them and know that you've missed the royal path to their hearts and minds. It's the difference between giving sermons that originate from your idea of what they should hear (formed mostly in the quiet of your study) and providing wake-up calls to the Bible's powerful relevance to the boisterous issues tearing people apart.

I'm always awed by the way Jesus was so adept in cutting to the chase, skipping the superfluous and driving home his point with exacting clarity. No obtuse speeches. No patronizing remarks. No long-winded, rambling monologues. Instead, he made every word count. Each statement was packed with meaning, masterfully wielded like a sword in the hands of a fencing champion. His message invariably pierced the heart with such accuracy that his listeners could not help but acknowledge the truth. It sent them over the edge with frenzied rage, or it forced them to their knees in conviction. Either way, they were never blasé about what they heard. They didn't walk away thinking, "That was a nice sermon." No, they walked away brimming with excitement, or they left to plot their revenge.

If we, as followers of this same Christ, could capture even a semblance of that power of presentation, it could revolutionize our impact. It's not about shouting or making dramatic gestures; it's about the power and succinctness of carefully chosen words. As one pastor put it, we are called to be radical without being fanatical.

INTRODUCING THE UNEXPECTED

Sometimes, being radical is what it takes to awaken the spiritually slumbering soul, much like the unexpected, which has a similar therapeutic effect in the counseling room. Interventions which reframe or restructure reality have a way of shaking up old patterns of thinking, prompting actions never considered before.

I recently had a Christian client who could not let go of his bitterness toward a former colleague who had gotten him fired from his job several years earlier. This bitterness had almost flat lined his spiritual life. I asked him if he had ever thought about the fact that his experience of betrayal was perhaps the closest he'd ever come to learning what Jesus might have humanly felt when Peter betrayed him. His eyes widened. "Ironically, you've been given a privilege few people have had," I observed. I further suggested he reread Jesus' response to Peter in John 21:15–17 and ask himself why Jesus didn't reject him. When he came back two weeks later, he was brimming with newfound insight about his Lord and excited to get back into the Word. Coincidentally, he released his bitterness as well.

Injecting the element of surprise into your ministry—and into your sermons—can also be a stimulating countermeasure to the deadening character of so many people's routine thinking. If you've been depressed before, you already know that constant sameness can kill the human spirit and dull the voice of the Holy Spirit. Periodically shaking things up can be useful as a refresher course on how to revitalize your life—and that of your church. Doing something different, or reframing it in a different way is the tonic that lets others know that they don't have to settle for something less than what God intended. Resignation doesn't envision new beginnings; it's merely toughing life out, waiting for the end.

Once again, we have a two-for-one sale on tools to avoid depression and, at the same time, to provide a spiritual facelift for your congregation.

9

KNOWING YOUR COMMUNITY

The broader community in which the church is embedded is a petri dish of culture, teeming with changing ideas and retooled experiments in social engineering. Some neighborhoods are undergoing urban renewal while others are decaying. There has been flight to the suburbs, followed by a return migration to the cities. Population (and therefore housing) density has dramatically increased, but government solvency has equally and dramatically decreased.

Even social interaction patterns have shifted. While homes of yesteryear had front porches from which neighbors chatted in amiable exchange, today we cherish our privacy, retreating to our decks behind our homes. Many are slowly replacing the familiar local bank teller with banking online, and soon the store clerk will fade in importance as shopping online or self-checkout begins to dominate. These and many other changes are at once exciting and uneasy transitions for everyone.

The churches have not escaped this revolution either. They have shed their massive pulpits and their impressive-sounding organs, now using stools on open stages and the music of contemporary bands. More formal wear is passé and casual wear is in—for the pastor as well as the congregation. There is still, of course, the small neighborhood church, but there is also today the reality of the megachurch where thousands of worshipers gather for services and everything is done on a grand scale. The advanced technology used in these services has filtered down to the local church as well.

NEW GENERATIONS AND NEW CHANGES

This kind of rapid change is the byword of the millennial generation. My son, who is a computer expert and lover of all things electronic, considers his cell phone, iPad, and PC as woefully obsolete if they are more than two years old. You can only imagine how he views my equipment—no doubt much like I view ten-inch-screen TVs with tin foil antennas. I don't offer much resistance though. After all, my computer fix-it guy is only a phone call away (though that may not be as impressive as it sounds if you saw the age of my cell phone). The point is that change—rapid, almost bewildering change—is now ingrained in the lexicon of culture and, therefore, in the local community.

Knowledge is exponentially increasing, roughly doubling every two years. In 1970 there was no Internet and no instant communication. Today, an estimated 1.3 billion people have an Internet connection and even more have satellite-driven cell phones. The medical sciences have advanced beyond all expectations. As a result, two-thirds of all people who have ever lived to age sixty-five are alive today. In our ability to destroy each other, the power of our weaponry has increased to such a point that one nuclear submarine can now deliver more explosive destruction than all the weapons of all the countries involved in World War II. We have lived through changes like these, and consequently, are awed by the differences. But young people have grown up with this pace of development and think there is little unusual about it.

THE DOWNSIDE OF CONTEMPORARY CULTURAL CHANGE

With such changes, however, has also come a disturbing trend: Young people are dropping out of the church at alarming rates. Part of this may be due to the lack of meaningful attachment to others and the failure to engage in anything of substance. Here we see the dramatic effects of the current decline of marriage and the family. In his epic tome on the state of American culture, professor Allan Bloom of the University of Chicago had this to say:

The decay of the family means that community would require extreme self-abnegation in an era when there is no good reason for anything but self-indulgence. . . . In the state of nature concerning friendships and love today, there is doubt about both, and the result is a longing for the vanished common ground, called roots. . . . The young want to make commitments, which constitute the meaning of life. . . . This is what they talk about, but they are haunted by the awareness that the talk does not mean much and that commitments are lighter than air.[1]

In a society where the core values of the family are rapidly losing ground and where parents have little more to say to their children other than they hope they will have a better life, Dr. Bloom delivers his most poignant observation: "The moral education that is today supposed to be the great responsibility of the family cannot exist if it cannot present to the imagination of the young the vision of a moral cosmos and of the rewards and punishments for good and evil."[2]

This, it seems, is the most profound point of entry for the church. Coupling the moral vacuity of the culture with young people's yearning for attachments that seem to elude them, the church has its best opportunity to lay out a vision that includes something secular society can't teach—what truly meaningful relationships actually look like. It's the chance to educate young people as to how a Christ-centered life stacks up to a secular one on the issues that matter to them most. It's important, however, to accurately present the secular point of view with the logic it employs, not a caricature of it, or the church will have little credibility in their eyes. They need to hear their own experience given a new explanation that makes sense to them, or else they will merely dismiss it as useless, inauthentic, Christian hyperventilation.

CONFRONTING THE UTOPIAN MYTH

Most people, especially young people, give extraordinary credence to their own point of view, because that is the way the world looks through their eyes. They may even assume that everyone else, at least the ones in their peer group, see it the same way. Because professors they admire for their intellect teach them the principles of socialist thinking, they are strongly wedded to a utopianism that has little correlation to the grim facts on the ground. But they think it is true really only because they want it to be.

Such utopianism was relatively foreign to the post-war boomer generation. It was only after the cultural revolution of the 1960s that the philosophies of eighteenth-century

Enlightenment thinking, which had been simmering in academia for nearly two hundred years, spilled out on to Main Street America. It now shapes many of the policies even of the local community. The slogan of the Vietnam War protest movement, "Make love, not war," perfectly encapsulated the utopian spirit. It promoted the belief that people's inherent goodness, if unleashed by destroying Western civilization and rebuilding it, would lead at last to a life without conflict. It would also lead to a life without the necessity of religion, which was (and is) seen as the source of most wars.

Have you ever wondered why, after Christ's second coming, the book of Revelation describes a thousand-year reign, after which the Evil One will be released for one final confrontation with God and his followers? Why not bring history to a close when Jesus victoriously returns to reign on earth? Isn't that enough? Notice that after the thousand years of perfect peace led by the perfect King, when Satan comes calling again, there will be an entire host of his minions willing to answer the call. In other words, even after experiencing Christ's loving reign, these secretly sinful people will still rebel the first chance they get. But of course they will be no match for God's sovereign power and will finally be destroyed.

Here you have, in the biblical record, the ultimate argument against false utopianism. Even under perfect (utopian) conditions, where there is no crime, there are no wars, in fact no conflict at all, there will still be evil lurking in the hearts of those who refuse to accept Christ's headship. Contrary to the utopian point of view, humanity, if left to its own devices, will never achieve the peace so loudly trumpeted. There will always be violence and unrest. Deny it if they will, but there is no substitute for God's love.

So the Bible itself takes on the very issue that most animates the culture today. How can we effectively address the issues of our communities without challenging the culture in which it is embedded? In a culture that is increasingly hostile to Christianity, the church has the opportunity to present a contrasting message of eternal meaning that poses an alternative to dependence on others to make life meaningful for us.

ACTION-BASED FAITH

To underscore its authenticity to the people, our message of hope must also develop legs by providing a concrete program of outreach to the community that demonstrates God's love in action. This requires the church to accurately target the needs and demographics of their communities. If you don't really know the local community, you cannot hope to serve it effectively. Conducting public surveys, individually interviewing neighbors and community leaders, holding meetings of common interest to those living near the church, and keeping careful watch of the local newspapers are all potentially useful means to measure the heartbeat of your community. What's important is that members of the community know you're intensely interested in them.

Author Tim Keller speaks to the issue of poverty in a similar framework. In fact, he argues persuasively for the importance of fulfilling the many biblical injunctions urging believers to address the plight of the needy. By doing so, he rightly identifies action-based empathy for the poor as a benchmark of authentic faith. It's in this sense, in particular, that the church cannot afford to be indifferent to the needs of those around it. To buttress his case, Keller cites the work of pastor Mike Gornik of New Song Church in the seedy Sandtown area of Baltimore, Maryland, as well as the renowned ministry of John M. Perkins in Mississippi and in the urban area of Los Angeles. These pastors have sought to lift poor people out of their persistent state of dependency and to actually help them learn how to lead self-sufficient lives.

Pastor Keller notes that, as far back as the Roman Empire, it was recognized that despite the specter of persecution, the fledgling Christian church continued to attract new converts, largely because of its generous spirit toward the poor. It's a case of people acknowledging their overwhelming spiritual debt reaching out to people with overwhelming material debt: "To the degree that the gospel shapes your self-image, you will identify with those in need. . . . When Christians who understand the gospel see a poor person, they realize they are looking into a mirror. Their hearts must go out to him or her without an ounce of superiority or indifference."[3]

Not only does this increase the effectiveness of your ministry, it also provides the stage upon which to publicly acknowledge the importance of humble service to others. And it is consciously serving others in need that keeps your mind on the transforming power of God, not on the frustrating misfires of others. Besides, focusing outwardly and upwardly is always a better strategy than fixating inwardly and negatively if you want to prevent depression and burnout.

That's the beauty of God's plan—while he's working *through* you to bring others into the kingdom, he's also working *in* you to strengthen you spiritually and emotionally for the task. You are called to do God's work but, in the doing, keep in touch with his voice. It will keep you from letting the good become an enemy of the best, from letting the other voices clamoring for your attention drown out the greater voice of wisdom.

NOTES

1. Allan Bloom, *The Closing of the American Mind* (New York: Simon & Schuster, 1987), 86, 109.

2. Ibid., 60.

3. Timothy Keller, *Generous Justice: How God's Grace Makes Us Just* (New York: Penguin, 2010), 102–103.

If you've benefited from reading this pastor's guide, check out *Light in the Darkness: Finding Hope in the Shadow of Depression* (WPH) by Gary H. Lovejoy, PhD, and Gregory M. Knopf, MD, available November 2014.

Hope for Congregation Members Wrestling with Depression

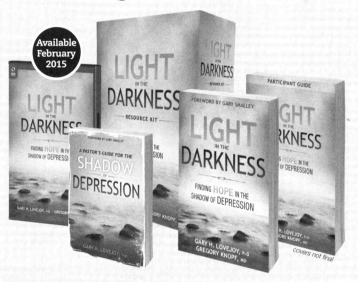

Available February 2015

covers not final

The Light in the Darkness Group Resource Kit provides everything you need to lead a group of congregation members through an in-depth study of Dr. Gary Lovejoy and Dr. Gregory Knopf's practical and hopeful book, *Light in the Darkness: Finding Hope in the Shadow of Depression*. It's also a great way to reach out to people in your community who may be experiencing depression. The group resource kit includes:

- 1 *Light in the Darkness: Finding Hope in the Shadow of Depression* book
- 1 *A Pastor's Guide for the Shadow of Depression* book
- 1 Light in the Darkness DVD (includes 13 video segments, 1 per chapter)
- 6 copies of *Light in the Darkness Participant Guide*
- Light in the Darkness Leader's Guide (free download)

Light in the Darkness Group Resource Kit
978-0-89827-827-9

Light in the Darkness

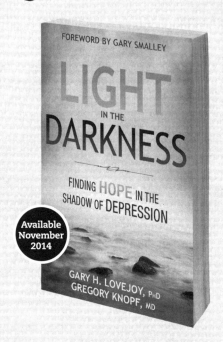

Many Christians struggle with the dark shadows depression can cast over our lives. Too often, our depression is compounded by a sense of personal shame or guilt. *Light in the Darkness* shows us how depression is actually a signal, warning us of emotional damage that needs repair. Here, readers will find a blueprint for restoring emotional health and rekindling the hope of faith that is both biblically and psychologically sound.

Light in the Darkness
978-0-89827-825-5
978-0-89827-826-2 (e-book)

1.800.493.7539 | WWW.WPHONLINE.COM